New Vanguard • 29

German Armoured Cars and Reconnaissance Half-Tracks 1939–45

Bryan Perrett • Illustrated by Bruce Culver and Jim Laurier

First published in Great Britain in 1999 by Osprey Publishing,
Midland House, West Way, Botley, Oxford OX2 0PH, UK
443 Park Avenue South, New York, NY 10016, USA
Email: info@ospreypublishing.com

© 1999 Osprey Publishing Ltd

Revised edition of Vanguard 25

ISBN 1 85532 849 6

CIP Data for this publication is available from the British Library
Military Editor: Marcus Cowper
Design: Chris@D4Design
Colour plates by Bruce Culver
Cutaway artwork by Jim Laurier
Cutaway annotation by Hilary Doyle

Origination by Valhaven Ltd, Isleworth, UK
Printed in China through World Print Ltd.

05 06 07 08 09   10 9 8 7 6

FOR A CATALOGUE OF ALL BOOKS PUBLISHED BY
OSPREY MILITARY AND AVIATION PLEASE CONTACT:

NORTH AMERICA
Osprey Direct, 2427 Bond Street,
University Park, IL 60466, USA
E-mail: info@ospreydirectusa.com

ALL OTHER REGIONS
Osprey Direct UK, P.O. Box 140,
Wellingborough, Northants, NN8 2FA, UK
E-mail: info@ospreydirect.co.uk

www.ospreypublishing.com

Acknowledgements

The author wishes to express his thanks to Oberst a.D. Helmut Ritgen and to
Oberst a.D. Fabian von Bonin von Ostau for their most generous advice and
assistance.

Editor's note

This book is a revised edition of Vanguard 25 *German Armoured Cars and
Reconnaissance Vehicles 1939–45*, first published in 1982. The text has been
revised, new black and white photos included and a detailed cutaway of an
SdKfz 234 added.

Artist's Note

Jim Laurier would like to thank the Patton Museum of Cavalry and Armor,
Fort Knox, Kentucky, USA, for their kind help in supplying reference material
for the annotated cutaway.

Readers may care to note that copies of the centre cutaway are available for
private sale: all reproduction copyright whatsoever is retained by the
Publishers. All enquiries should be addressed to:

Jim Laurier, PO Box 1118, Keene, NH 03431 USA
http://aviation-art.simplenet.com

The Publishers regret that they can enter into no correspondence upon
this matter.

GERMAN ARMOURED CARS AND RECONNAISSANCE HALF-TRACKS 1939–45

DEVELOPMENT

At the turn of the century the Imperial German General Staff, despite its undoubted brilliance, was, if anything, even more conservative in its outlook than its contemporaries, and was determined to win any future war with the three classic arms – cavalry, artillery and infantry. It viewed with dislike mechanical innovations which, in its view, created fresh and unnecessary problems which tended to detract from the main issue – and, of course, it was not alone in this. It was, however, an era in which immense progress was being made in the automotive field and, as in other countries, the War Ministry was bombarded with ideas from designers and manufacturers which had to be given a reasonable degree of consideration.

One of the earliest suggestions came from Kaiser Wilhelm himself. What he proposed was an immense armoured machine which was to be known as the 'Battle-Rank Breaker'. The vehicle ran on four wheels, was steam-powered, and resembled a double-decker tramcar with a chimney; the exterior bristled with spikes and contained nearly as many gun-ports as one of Nelson's frigates. Had it been built its ground-clearance would have been negligible and its ground-pressure quite insupportable. No doubt, after suitably polite comments had been made concerning *Sein Altesse's* gifted imagination, the idea was smartly steered into the nearest filing cabinet.

On the other hand, if the Kaiser's proposal lacked practicality, that made by Paul Daimler in 1904 certainly did not and indeed was several steps ahead of its time. His **Daimler Panzerwagen**, built at the Wiener-Neustadt works of the Österreiches Daimler Motoren AG, contained a number of advanced ideas including a domeshaped, rotating turret containing one and later two Maxim machine-guns; an enclosed hull; and four-wheel drive. The vehicle weighed three tons, had a maximum speed of 28mph and an operational radius of 155 miles. It was demonstrated at both the Imperial German and Austro-Hungarian Army manoeuvres of 1905, but was considered to have little practical application, although it performed well.

Rather more attention was attracted the following year by a demonstration of the **Panzer-kraftwagen Ehrhardt 5cm BAK (Ballon Abwehr Kanone)**. As its name implies, this vehicle had been designed for use against the tethered observation balloons which were now a universal feature of the battlefield, and it must have generated some interest among now elderly

A group of Freikorps officers and NCOs pose with a twin-turret armoured car shortly after the end of the First World War. A variety of types were used for internal security during this period. Interestingly, the officer in the centre wears a pilot's badge on his tunic, and on his left forearm a death's-head patch (an insignia used widely in the Freikorps movement) above a cuff-title: 'Kampfwagen'. (Imperial War Museum)

officers who, as young cavalrymen, had been involved in the fruitless pursuit of the hot-air balloons which had floated across their siege lines at Paris in 1870; again, Graf Zeppelin's experiments had shown that use of the dirigible airship for military purposes was probable, and other countries could be counted upon to follow the German lead. The Ehrhardt BAK was based on a light lorry chassis and powered by a 50hp engine; its capacity for high-angle fire was useful but was curbed by the limited traverse available, to the weapon, and a further fault lay in the provision of drive to the rear wheels only, which restricted mobility.

These defects were eliminated in the **Krupp-Daimler Panzerkraftwagen 5.7cm BAK**, which appeared in 1909, although in this case the ammunition racks were inconveniently sited for the gun crew. Solid tyres were fitted to the front wheels and pneumatic to the rear. The Panzerkraftwagen 5.7cm BAK is noted as having taken part in that year's Army manoeuvres.

In 1910 the Krupp-Daimler combination produced an unarmoured version of the BAK which it was decided to take into service, it being considered that armoured protection was superfluous to the role for which the vehicle had been designed. The BAKs were the first purpose-built anti-aircraft fighting vehicles and saw extensive service throughout the First World War, achieving some success. Fire control was largely a matter of inspired guesswork, but the targets flew so slowly and were of such flimsy construction that even a near miss with a shrapnel round could cause serious damage. It has been calculated that the entire flak system, mobile or otherwise, fired an average of 1,000 shells for each aircraft destroyed. When engaging high-angle targets the BAK had to be jacked down to prevent recoil pressures damaging the bed of the vehicle. Ground targets, too, could be engaged, and several BAKs took part in a far-sighted mechanised infantry operation in Rumania which accurately foreshadowed the role of the Panzergrenadier.

To all intents and purposes, therefore, the German Army entered the First World War without armoured cars; it was to be forced to invoke a degree of mechanisation. Speed, it will be recalled, was the essence of the Schlieffen Plan, and those formations on the outer edge of the gigantic wheel which pivoted on the Franco-German frontier obviously had to move further and faster than anyone else. This was particularly hard on the Jäger battalions attached to the cavalry divisions of the advanced screen, but their difficulty in keeping up with the horsemen had been foreseen and several, in part at least, had been issued with standard touring cars which had been given limited protection. These motorised detachments, which included machine-

Daimler Gepanzerter Mannschaftstransportwagen (SdKfz 3) of the Reichswehr on manoeuvres in East Prussia in 1928. These MTWs were unarmed armoured personnel carriers; under the Allied Control Commission regulations only the Schutzpolizei were permitted true armoured cars. (Bundesarchiv)

The futuristic Adler reconnaissance vehicle was protected by thin aluminium armour. This photo shows the Reconnaissance Troop of the 3rd (Prussian) Motorised Bn., commanded in 1930–31 by Heinz Guderian. (Bundesarchiv)

gun teams, frequently preceded the cavalry and seized important bridges, rail junctions and so on before the retreating French and Belgians could destroy them. Most of the details regarding these admittedly minor actions have unfortunately been lost in the telling of greater events.

Also attached to each cavalry division were two larger protected vehicles, weighing approximately ten tons, powered by Mercedes-Benz engines which could produce a top speed of 20mph on good going, and armed with either a light fieldpiece or machine-guns. Divisional commanders found little scope for the independent use of their armoured lorries, either on their own account or in support of the motorised Jäger detachments; instead, the vehicles seem to have been employed primarily for mobile fire support of the mounted squadrons.

Once the front became static these expedient vehicles took no further part in the fighting in the West, although some may have been transferred to the more fluid Eastern Front. One of the heavy type surfaced in Syria as late as 22 October 1918, when the LAMBs (Light Armoured Motor Batteries) leading Allenby's pursuit of the beaten Turkish armies to Aleppo encountered it near Khan Sebil, escorting a small motor convoy. For a while the Mercedes held its own, but its weight and solid tyres were a disadvantage in a running fight, causing it to lose ground on the slightest up-grade. With the nimbler Rolls-Royces rapidly closing the gap, the crew abandoned their vehicle. The armoured body was found to have withstood its opponents' fire, but the machine gun shield had been penetrated several times; nor had its difficulties been eased by the arrival of two Turkish aircraft, which had joined in the fight with a pronounced lack of discrimination.

The success of British and Belgian armoured car units during the opening moves of the war had sufficiently impressed the General Staff that in 1915 it decided, in a fairly leisurely way, to develop an armoured car branch of its own. The three manufacturers Daimler, Ehrhardt and Bussing were asked to produce designs which incorporated four-wheel drive, a generous ground clearance, and an additional rear-steering position which would enable the cars to be quickly reversed out of trouble.

The three prototypes, the **Panzerkraftwagen Daimler/15**, **Panzerkraftwagen Ehrhardt/15** and the **Panzerkraftwagen Bussing/15**, were all completed by the beginning of 1916, and provide interesting early examples of design overkill. They were of massive dimensions – the Bussing model was over 30 feet long – and lacked the wolfish elegance of the Rolls-Royce. They weighed 9–10 tons, were protected by 7–9mm armour, and were armed with three machine-guns, for which a number of alternative ports were provided in the static turret and hull.

In cost-effectiveness terms the number of crewmen carried – commander, two drivers and six gunners – was wildly extravagant.

The designs were approved and these vehicles formed the basis of the first German armoured car unit, Panzerkraftwagen Maschinengewehr Abteilung I (Motorised Armoured Machine Gun Battalion I). In 1916 this unit served at Verdun and elsewhere on the Western Front, and in the autumn of that year took part in the successful Rumanian campaign with General von Schmettow's cavalry corps.

An SdKfz 13 'Bathtub' of an infantry division's reconnaissance battalion photographed during the campaign in Poland. The solid white national cross provided too good an aiming mark and was subsequently overlaid in black. (RAC Tank Museum)

In July 1917 there took place what was probably the first duel fought between purpose-built armoured cars. During Kerensky's abortive July offensive Commander Oliver Locker Lampson's RNAS armoured car unit had supported Russian attacks on the Brzezany sector and had repeatedly carried out raids down the main road to enfilade the enemy trenches. On one occasion they found their way blocked by a large armoured car of unfamiliar design, and each side opened fire at 600 yards. Neither did the other any damage and the affair looked like ending in stalemate until a Seabrook Heavy, armed with a 3pdr. gun, was sent up to assist the battling Lanchesters. At this, the enemy machine reversed into its own lines. At some personal risk, one of the RNAS men sketched the German car; the result was hardly representative, but his drawing does show a long, four-wheeled vehicle of symmetrical design, a description which could only apply to the Bussing.

For the remainder of the war technical development and the expansion of the armoured car branch proceeded very slowly. In 1917 Ehrhardt produced an improved version of their 1915 model, incorporating a rotating turret and reducing the vehicle's weight by 1.75 tons. Some were fitted with a radio which could only be used when halted; this bulky addition was not popular with crews, already crowded to the point of claustrophobia, but was a marked step forward in the use of cars as armoured observation posts. The initial production run was used to form Panzerkraftwagen Maschinengewehr Zuge 2, 3, 4, 5 and 6, each of which consisted of two armoured cars and supporting transport.

The Inter-war Years

The Armistice left Germany in an extremely unsettled state. A Spartacist rising took place in Berlin, there were organised disturbances elsewhere, and German interests along the country's eastern frontiers were threatened by Bolshevik influences. Throughout this period the Daimler, Ehrhardt and Bussing armoured cars, together with some locally armoured civilian vehicles, were kept fully employed by the security forces and by the Freikorps, which were groups of former officers and soldiers who had volunteered for further service until order could be restored; it was unfortunate that some Freikorps commanders, by their excessive behaviour, brought suspicion on what was essentially a patriotic movement.

The terms of the Versailles Treaty of 1920 ensured nothing but the inevitability of a second world war. The military clauses provided for a reduction of the Army's overall strength to 100,000 men, and that of the officer corps from 40,000 to 4,000. Naturally, only the best were retained and these were trained to think two steps ahead of their actual rank so that when the time came for expansion the enlarged Army would be a very efficient organisation indeed. A further and unforeseen effect of this reduction was to concentrate the best military brains into what was in effect a large think-tank, which carried out a critical analysis of the technical reasons for Germany's defeat and studied in depth the implications of the new mechanised warfare, particularly the theories of British writers on the subject.

For the moment, however, little could be done to test the viability of these theories, for the military clauses also forbade the Army any sort of armoured vehicle apart from a few wheeled personnel carriers. These were built by Daimler under the designation **Gepanzerter Mannschaftstransportwagen (SdKfz 3)** (or MTW) and resembled the firm's armoured car save that they were completely unarmed and lacked rear-steering. They carried a crew of three and a section of 12 riflemen and were issued at the scale of 15 to each of the Reichswehr's seven motor battalions.

However, as an aid to the civil power, the government had established a 150,000-strong armed force known as the Schutzpolizei, the administration of which was decentralised among the various German states. After the disturbances of 1918–1919 the Allied Control Commission had no objection to Schutzpolizei operations being supported by armoured cars, although they limited the number to one per 1,000 men. The cars, described as **Schutzpolizei Sonderwagen** (Armed Police Special Purpose Vehicles), more commonly shortened to Sonderschupowagen, were built by Daimler, Ehrhardt and Benz; they had twin machine-gun turrets, a command cupola and rear-steering. Had hostilities broken out there can be little doubt that the Army would have been quick to lay hands on them, and a few did in fact mysteriously find their way into military service.

It was now quite apparent that horsed cavalry had only a limited use in its traditional reconnaissance role, and that that role would increasingly be carried out by armoured cars. In predicting its future requirements the Reichswehr did not favour the First World War or Sonderschupowagen designs, which were more suitable for street fighting, and concentrated instead on the development of a vehicle with high-speed cross-country performance. The activities of

SdKfz 13 ('Bathtub') scout cars during the 1936 Army Manoeuvres: the dachshund is not impressed. (Bundesarchiv)

SdKfz 222 light armoured car with anti-grenade grilles open. This vehicle, photographed in N. Africa, carries the standard armament of one 20mm cannon and one 7.92mm machine-gun; it is sprayed overall in sand yellow, but the inside of the hatch shows the original 'Panzer grey'. (RAC Tank Museum)

the Control Commission inhibited work inside Germany, and many of the practical aspects were resolved at the secret testing station set up at Kazan in Russia under the secret terms of the Russo-German Rapallo Agreement. Three firms participated, describing their vehicles as trial replacements for the MTW; Daimler-Benz and Magirus each produced an **ARW** (Achtradwagen or eight-wheeled vehicle) with drive to each wheel and duplicate fore and aft controls, while Bussing offered a **ZRW** (Zehnradwagen or ten-wheeled vehicle) with similar facilities. Continued development along these promising lines was interrupted by the world economic crisis, which hit Germany particularly hard, although the lessons learned were put to good use later.

By the turn of the decade the MTWs had been replaced or supplemented by another wheeled personnel carrier, a lightly armoured version of the four-wheeled Adler Standard-6 lorry fitted with a rotating cupola which contained a machine-gun. These vehicles seem to have been employed as scout cars and are known to have equipped the Reconnaissance Platoon of the 3rd (Prussian) Motorised Battalion which, during the period 1930–1931, was commanded by the then-Oberstleutnant Heinz Guderian.

The Adler 4 x 2-wheel drive also served as the basis for a light, open-topped scout car, the **SdKfz 13**, which mounted a single machine-gun. This vehicle, known for obvious reasons as 'The Bathtub', was protected by 8mm armour and carried a crew of two. Its top speed of 31 mph was unimpressive, as was its cross-country performance. It entered service with the cavalry in 1933, but by the start of the Second World War had been relegated to the heavy squadron of the infantry divisions' reconnaissance battalions. The Polish campaign confirmed its unsuitability for first line use and it was subsequently employed on internal security duties in occupied countries. A wireless version, the **SdKfz 14**, was fitted with a frame aerial and carried an extra crew member.

Work on the Bathtub's replacement began in 1935 and resulted two years later in the appearance of the **SdKfz 221** light armoured car. This vehicle was the first German armoured car to employ a rear mounting for its engine, a 75hp Horch, and had a maximum speed of 46mph. It had four-wheel drive, four-wheel steering and an independent coil-spring suspension. It was protected by 14.5mm angled armour and a small, open-topped turret mounted a 7.92mm machine-gun; in some later versions the machine-gun was replaced by a 2.8cm Panzerbuchse, the name given to a tapered-bore anti-tank rifle. The crew consisted of commander and driver.

The **SdKfz 222** light armoured car was developed directly from the 221 and began entering service with armoured reconnaissance battalions in 1938. The principal improvement on the basic design was the provision of a larger turret mounting a 20mm cannon co-axially with a 7.92mm machine-gun, although again some versions were armed with the 2.8cm Panzerbuchse; as with the 221, the turret was open-topped, but some protection was provided against grenades by hinged wire grilles which could be closed over the commander's head. Some vehicles were fitted with radio sets, although these lacked the 20mm cannon. The 222 was built in far greater numbers than the 221 and is probably the best remembered German light armoured car of the Second World War. Its crew consisted of commander, driver and, on wireless versions, an operator.

The series based on this chassis was extended by the three-man **SdKfz 223 Panzerspähwagen (Fu)** – Armoured Scout Car (Radio) – which appeared about the same time as the 222. It employed the 222 hull but had a much smaller turret mounting a single 7.92mm machine-gun, and carried a wireless set as standard equipment, together with a collapsible frame aerial.

Detail of the 20mm mounting and anti-grenade grilles of an SdKfz 222 – the co-axial MG is absent. (RAC Tank Museum)

Last in the series were two turretless command vehicles, the **SdKfz 260** and **SdKfZ 261 Kleiner Panzerfunkwagen** (Light Armoured Radio Vehicles) which were based on the hull of the 221. The 260 carried rod aerials and the 261 a frame aerial; both had a crew consisting of commander, driver and two operators.

In general, the vehicles of this series were fast and manoeuvrable during road use, but performed poorly across country. Production was discontinued in 1942, although many light armoured cars remained in service until the end of the war. Sometimes classed simply as the Horch series, their components were actually produced by a number of manufacturers and assembled by the firm of Schichau at Elbing and by Maschinenfabrik Niedersachsen at Hannover-Linden.

Meanwhile a series of heavy armoured cars had been developed concurrently. Design work had begun in 1930, taking the Daimler G3 6 x 4 commercial vehicle chassis as a starting point. This led directly to the appearance of the **SdKfz 231 Schwere Panzerspähwagen (6-rad)** – Heavy Armoured Car, six–wheeled – in 1932. The vehicle's civilian ancestry was evident in its front-engined layout, and only the two rear axles were driven; steering was obtained through the front wheels only. A rear-steering position incorporated driver's controls as well as a steering wheel. Three types of engine were employed; a 68hp Daimler, a 70hp Magirus, or a 65hp Bussing, each giving an approximate top road-speed Of 37mph. The armour had a 14.5mm base and was well angled. The turret had all-round traverse and mounted a 20mm cannon coaxially with a 7.92mm machine-gun. A crew of four was carried.

A wireless version, the **SdKfz 232 Schwere Panzerspähwagen (6-rad) (Fu)**, was also developed, mounting a prominent 'bedstead' frame aerial on top of the vehicle. The aerial was attached to two fixed brackets at the rear of the hull, but incorporated a rotating central pivot from which arms descended to the turret, which thus retained all-round traverse. This equipment made the 232 slightly heavier than the 231 (6.15 tons as opposed to 5.9 tons).

A command vehicle, the **SdKfz 263 Panzerfunkwagen (6-rad)**, closely resembled the 232 but had a fixed turret mounting a single 7.92mm machine-gun. This weighed 5.75 tons and carried a crew of five.

An interesting feature of the six-wheeled designs was the provision of ground rollers. One roller was suspended beneath the nose of the vehicle to prevent it embedding in steep slopes or in the far banks of ditches; a second was fitted to the underside of the chassis between the fore and aft wheels to prevent the hull grounding. Even so, cross-country performance was poor, mainly because of the lack of drive to the front axle.

These vehicles, always regarded as interim designs, served in the armoured reconnaissance battalions, and some took part in the Polish and French campaigns of 1939 and 1940 before being withdrawn from service or relegated to internal security duties in occupied countries.

The experience gained with the experimental Achtradwagen and the defects revealed in the operational performance of the six-wheelers greatly assisted the Heereswaffen-amt, responsible for pro-curement, in deciding what sort of heavy armoured car was needed by the Army. The specification called for a rear-engined, eight-wheeled vehicle with front and rear driving positions

SdKfz 223 radio vehicle photographed shortly after the Afrika Korps' arrival in Libya, to judge by the use of the sun helmet and by the rather chaotic stowage. This car is evidently being used in the command role; a guyed pole aerial is employed as well as the standard frame aerial. (Bundesarchiv)

SdKfz 222 in Tunisia, 1943; after two years of desert warfare neat, workmanlike stowage has become a matter of routine. A few fronds of greenery have been added to the vehicle's camouflage, as the Tunisian spring has changed the overall aspect of the landscape. (Bundesarchiv)

and drive and steering on all wheels. Deutsche Werk of Kiel were made responsible for the vehicle's development in 1935, while assembly of the standardised design was carried out by the Schichau organisation.

The new car began replacing the SdKfz 231 (6-rad) in the armoured reconnaissance battalions in 1938. Somewhat confusingly, its designation was **SdKfz 231 Schwere Panzerspähwagen (8-rad)**, it being contemporary practice to apply the Sonderkraftfahrzeug (special purpose vehicle) number to the vehicle's role rather than to its design, to which the only reference lay in mention of the wheel arrangement.

The 231 (8-rad) weighed 8.15 tons and was powered by a Bussing 155hp (later increased to 180hp) engine which produced a maximum road-speed of 53mph. As might be expected, the transmission and line-of-drive design was complex. Independent longitudinal leaf springs provided the suspension for each wheel, and cross-country performance could be compared to that of a tracked vehicle. A distinctive recognition feature was the mudguard arrangement, each shield covering two wheels.

A 14.5mm basis was employed for the steeply angled armour, the thickness of the frontal armour being subsequently increased to 30mm. The turret was armed with a 20mm cannon mounted co-axially with a 7.92mm machine-gun. The radio version, **SdKfz 232 Schwere Panzerspähwagen (8-rad) (Fu)**, carried a similar frame aerial to that of the SdKfz 232 (6-rad) and was 0.2 tons heavier. Like the 231 (8-rad) the vehicle was manned by a crew of four, and was armed with a 20mm cannon and co-axial machine-gun.

A turretless command vehicle, the **SdKfz 262 Panzerfunkwagen (8-rad)**, was also developed, the height of the hull being raised slightly to protect the five-man crew. A static frame aerial was fitted, being replaced during the war years by simpler rod aerials, as was that of the SdKfz 232 (8rad). Provision was made for the mounting of a single machine-gun, but this was not always carried. Both the six- and eightwheeled versions of the SdKfz 263 served in the signals sections of the armoured reconnaissance battalions, and also with armoured signals battalions.

Wartime Designs

Last to appear in this series was another turretless vehicle, the **SdKfz 233 Schwere Panzerspähwagen 75mm**. This entered service in 1941 and was employed in the close-support role, being armed with a 75mm L/24 howitzer. This was mounted at the front of the open-topped fighting compartment, but only a limited traverse was available; no secondary armament seems to have been carried. The 233 replaced the towed 75mm howitzer in the heavy squadrons of the armoured reconnaissance battalions. The eight-wheeled 231–233 series remained in service throughout the war, but production was discontinued in 1942.

With no little prescience, since Germany had yet to become involved in the North African campaign, the Heereswaffenamt initiated design work in August 1940 on a heavy armoured car intended for service in hot climates. The Czech firm of Tatra were asked to produce an air-cooled V-12 diesel engine with an Output of 220hp, and the prototype of this was ready by the end of 1941. The Bussing organisation was made responsible for the hull, which closely resembled that of the 231 (8-rad), but was of monocoque construction and thus dispensed with the need for a separate chassis; Daimler-Benz and Schichau were jointly responsible for the turret. The design was standardised as **Sdkfz 234/1 Schwere Panzerspähwagen (8-rad)** in 1943 and went into mass production in July of that year. Increased fuel capacity gave an operational radius which was approximately twice that of the 231 (8-rad) series, and the use of larger diameter tyres produced an outstanding cross-country performance. At 10.33 tons the vehicle was some 20 per cent heavier than the 231, but its maximum road speed was only marginally less.

The thickness of hull and turret frontal armour was 30mm; turret side and rear armour was 14.5mm, with 8mm side armour on the hull and 10mm on the rear. The turret was open-topped but was fitted with protective mesh cages similar to those mounted on the 222 light armoured car. Armament consisted of one 20mm cannon mounted co-axially with a 7.92mm machine-gun; radio was now fitted as standard. The vehicle was manned by a crew of four.

The most common complaint amongst German armoured car crewmen was that when they were forced to engage, their armament was frequently less than adequate. This imbalance was corrected to some degree in the **SdKfz 234/2 Schwere Panzerspähwagen (50mm) Puma**, which mounted the same KwK 39 50mm L/60 gun carried by the PzKpfw III Ausfs. J and L, with the very necessary addition of a muzzle brake. The gun, for which 55 rounds of ammunition were stowed, was housed co-axially with a 7.92mm machine-gun in a cramped but enclosed turret with all-round traverse, entering through a prominent bell-shaped external mantlet. This arrangement added half a ton to the weight of the basic 234 design, the penalty being a slight reduction in the maximum speed obtainable.

A turretless close-support version, the **SdKfz 234/3 Schwere Panzerspähwagen 75mm**, was also produced, armed with a 75mm L/24 howitzer; the sides of the fighting compartment were raised to protect the crew. As with the 233 (8-rad), only a limited degree of traverse was available.

The 234 series might have ended there had it not been for Hitler's insistence that it be extended with a further turretless variant, the **SdKfz 234/4 Schwere Panzerspähwagen 75mm**. This involved mounting the complete 75mm PAK 40 anti-tank gun, less wheels, on a pivot in the centre of the fighting compartment. The effect of this was to turn the vehicle into a wheeled tank destroyer but, once again, full use of the weapon was inhibited by the limited traverse obtainable.

Altogether, some 2,300 vehicles of the 234 type were built. Ironically, by the time they entered service the North African campaign had been over for many months; but the Tatra engine performed just as efficiently in extreme cold as in extreme heat, and the vehicles stood up well to the rigours of eastern European winters. The series represented one of the most advanced concepts in wheeled fighting vehicle design to appear during the Second World War. Sometimes confused with the 231–233 (8-rad) series, it is easily identified by the one-piece mudguard running the length of the hull containing various stowage bins and lockers.

A further enterprising design was a private venture on the part of Trippelwerke of Molsheim. This was the **Schildkrote** ('Turtle') 4 x 4 amphibious scout car, of which three experimental versions were built armed with a 7.92mm machine-gun or a 20mm cannon, or both. The project was abandoned in 1942 without a production order being received from the Heereswaffenamt. The vehicle's major defects included thin 10mm armour, the maximum that could be carried if buoyancy was to be preserved, but nonetheless inadequate; and the unsatisfactory performance of the Tatra V-8 petrol engine.

While not an armoured car in the true sense – nor indeed a reconnaissance vehicle at all – some mention must be made of the **SdKfz 247 Armoured Staff Car**. These vehicles were based on the standard 6 x 4 military chassis, which was itself an extension of a Krupp commercial cross-country design, and were built in small numbers only. Their primary use was to convey senior officers around particularly exposed sectors of the front.

Little use was made of armoured cars manufactured by satellite countries occupied by Germany before the outbreak of the Second World War, although the Austrian Saurer wheel-cum-track was taken into service in small numbers, equipped with radio, and designated **SdKfz 254 Mittlerer Gepanzerter Beobachtungskraftwagen** (Medium Armoured Artillery Observation Vehicle). The Austro-Daimler ADGZ 8 x 8 armoured car of 1934 also saw limited service, mainly in the internal security role. The ADGZ was of completely symmetrical design with front and rear driving positions, and was armed with three 20mm cannons, one in the turret and one in each of the bow plates. Steering was obtained through the fore and aft wheels only, but an interesting feature was that the track of' the four centre wheels lay outside these, so providing a greater area of tractive effort in bad going. The vehicle carried an over-large crew of 6–7 and had a maximum road speed of 44mph. Armoured protection was limited to 11mm.

Following the fall of France, some 190 of the excellent Panhard 178 4 x 4 armoured cars were taken into German service under the designation **Panzerspähwagen P204 (f)**. Of these, 150 were distributed among the armoured reconnaissance battalions where their 25mm gun (mounted co-axially with a machine-gun) provided a punch that had previously been lacking. The Panhard weighed 8.2 tons and was powered by a 105hp two-stroke petrol engine which produced a top speed of 50mph. The vehicle was protected by 20mm armour and manned by a crew of four.

The remaining 40 vehicles were converted for railway use by the removal of their road wheels and the substitution of flanged steel wheels. They were fitted with radio and for a time carried frame

Light armoured cars awaiting rail transport to the front, summer 1942, protected by the rail-head's permanent overhead canopies from enemy aerial observation. Closest to the camera are two SdKfz 223s with an SdKfz 261 Kleiner Panzerfunkwagen between them; further down the line are several SdKfz 222s. (Martin Windrow)

aerials. Their roles included straightforward reconnaissance along railways, and acting as scouts for other rail traffic in areas subject to partisan interference.

Extensive use was also made of captured armoured cars. These presented only a fraction of the technical problems associated with taking captured tanks into service, and their employment could provide a bonus in a role the major part of which lay in stealth and deception. Among enemy vehicles to be found serving in German armoured reconnaissance battalions were various Russian types, the British Daimler scout car and Humber armoured car, the South African Marmon-Herrington, the American M8, and, after the Italian surrender, the Fiat 40.

Reconnaissance Half-tracks

From 1942 onwards the equipment of the armoured reconnaissance battalions underwent a drastic revision. The reasons for this were two-fold: first, the Russian winter rains and spring thaw – the *rasputitsa* – made cross-country movement almost impossible for wheeled vehicles, and simultaneously the bottom dropped out of the unsurfaced tracks which constituted most of Russia's road network. The eight-wheeled cars coped, with difficulty, but the smaller four-wheeled cars were left floundering until towed free or dug out. Secondly, casualties among the reconnaissance battalions' motor-cycle troops had been heavier than anticipated, and a safer method of bringing the motor riflemen into action had to be found.

The answer to both problems appeared in the form of the **SdKfz 250 Leichter Schutzenpanzerwagen** (Light Armoured Personnel Carrier) series, which had been under development by the Demag organisation since 1940 as a smaller and nimbler complement to the SdKfz 251

Perhaps the most famous 250 of all Rommel's personal command vehicle 'Greif' (Griffin) passing through infantry outposts on the fringe of a tank battle in N. Africa, 1942. Note extra racks for jerrycans welded on the rear hull. (Bundesarchiv)

SdKfz 250/1 with suspension problems: Russia, autumn 1941. The use of hammer and cold chisel seems to imply stones jammed between the bogies, a common complaint of interleaved suspensions. The long bonnet of the 250 series gave a large reflective area, which this crew have countered by applying a thick coat of mud. The left-hand man wears what seems to be the assault artillery uniform; later in the war some recce units seem to have adopted it, with suitable changes of insignia. (Bundesarchiv)

Mittlerer Schutzenpanzerwagen series. Strictly speaking a three-quarter track, the 250 weighed 5.61 tons and was powered by a front-mounted 100hp Maybach engine which produced a maximum speed of 37mph. An interleaved suspension was employed for the tracked portion of the vehicle, the drive being transmitted to the track by way of a front sprocket. The track itself was self-lubricating and padded with rubber to deaden noise. Both the engine and fighting compartments were protected by 12mm angled armour plate. What made the 250 particularly suitable for reconnaissance work were its low height – only 5ft. 6ins. to the top of the hull – which enabled it to take advantage of even limited cover, and the obvious improvement in cross-country performance it provided over the light armoured car series. It was therefore entirely logical in the prevailing circumstances that the 250 should supplant the four-wheeled cars and also absorb the duties of the battalions' motor rifle element as well. Altogether, twelve versions of the 250 were produced, as follows:

SdKfz 250/1 Leichter Schutzenpanzerwagen	
SdKfz 250/2 Fernsprechwagen	Telephone vehicle
SdKfz 250/3 Funkwagen	Radio vehicle
SdKfz 250/4 Luftschutzwagen	Air support vehicle
SdKfz 250/5 Beobachtungswagen	Artillery observation post vehicle
SdKfz 250/6 Munitionswagen	Ammunition and supply carrier
SdKfz 250/7 80mm Granatwerferwagen	80mm mortar carrier
SdKfz 250/8 75mm L/24 auf le SPW	Self-propelled 75mm L/24 howitzer
SdKfz 250/9 Panzerspähwagen	Armoured reconnaissance vehicle
SdKfz 250/10 37mm PAK auf le SPW	Self-propelled 37mm anti-tank gun
SdKfz 250/11 sPzB 41 auf le SPW	Self-propelled 28mm Panzerbuchse
SdKfz 250/12 le Messtrupp Panzerwagen	Armoured survey section vehicle

Several of these variants, of course, had little to do with reconnaissance. The 250/2 telephone vehicle, for example, was a field telephone line-layer which could also mount a switchboard, and was designed for use by infantry and Panzergrenadier divisions in static or semi-static situations.

The 250/4 air support vehicle was used by Luftwaffe ground-attack controllers with radio sets netted to the aircraft frequency. Normally these officers worked with the main body of the formations to which they were attached; on the other hand, since Luftwaffe policy placed almost as much emphasis on interdiction tasks behind enemy lines (i.e. the prevention of reinforcement and supply movement) as on immediate tactical support, it would have been very strange had not the 250/4 accompanied the reconnaissance troops' deep penetration missions from time to time.

Both the 250/5 observation post vehicle and the 250/12 survey section vehicle had specialist artillery uses and were usually to be found in the Panzergrenadier divisions. The 250/5 carried radios netted both to the formation frequency and to that of the guns, an artillery plotting board, and high-power optical aids with which to observe the fall of shot. The 250/12 carried the survey party's levels, poles and markers necessary to establish the exact position of the batteries and other features.

The 250/1 armoured personnel carrier was, of course, employed in the Panzergrenadier role, but its widest application was with the armoured reconnaissance battalions, as was that of the 250/3 radio vehicle. The latter, fitted with an additional set, provided the reconnaissance squadron leader's link between his various troops forward and his own battalion headquarters. The 250/6 munitions carrier, the 250/7 80mm mortar carrier, the 250/8 self-propelled 75mm howitzer, the 250/10 self-propelled 37mm anti-tank gun and the 250/11 self-propelled Panzerbuchse were all eventually incorporated into the armoured reconnaissance battalion's order of battle. Perhaps the most interesting acquisition, however, was the 250/9 armoured reconnaissance vehicle, which was fitted with the turret of the 222 light armoured car, complete with armament; as will be seen from the official designation above, this vehicle was actually classed as an armoured car.

The size of crew carried by the 250 series varied according to its role, the 250/1 being manned by six but the 250/9 by only three. Further developments utilising the same chassis were the **SdKfz 252** munitions carrier and the **SdKfz 253 Leichter Panzerbeobachtungswagen**, both of which had somewhat improved armour protection but which were built only in small numbers and are not strictly relevant to the theme.

Versatile though the 250 series might be, it was beyond denial that crews in the open-topped fighting compartments were extremely vulnerable to air-bursts, or indeed any kind of fire from above. Again, while the cross-country performance of the half-tracks was better than that of the four-wheeled cars, it was still below that of the eight-wheelers, and as early as October 1943 thoughts were turning towards the substitution of a fully tracked chassis in place of the 250s.

As the German armaments industry was now under intense pressure, the immediate choice fell upon the proven chassis of the now obsolete battle tank PzKpfw 38(t). The tank turret was removed and replaced by that of the 222 light armoured car and in this form the vehicle was standardised as **SdKfz 140/1 Aufklärungspanzer**

SdKfz 250/10 self-propelled 37mm anti-tank gun mounting; note MG 34 on rear pintle. The 37mm gun was not highly regarded by its users, being termed 'The Military Door-Knocker'. (Bundesarchiv)

38(t) (Reconnaissance Tank 38(t)). Seventy of these conversions were made and issued in 1944, but no further developments took place along these lines, and this was the last reconnaissance vehicle to enter service with the German Army before the war ended.

ORGANISATION AND METHOD

In an armoured regiment equal priority is placed upon the characteristics of firepower, protection, mobility and flexibility. In an armoured reconnaissance battalion these priorities do not have equal weight and their order of precedence may, in lay eyes, appear somewhat unusual. The battalion's entire *raison d'etre* rests upon the gathering of information for its parent formation, and for this task the abstract quality of flexibility is the prime requirement, especially during the planning phase and in the field of radio communication; the radio is the reconnaissance vehicle's most important weapon, and its use can cause untold damage. Therefore mobility is equally essential to transport it into its operation area. However, occasions may arise when the information sought has to be fought for, and in this context some protection and firepower is useful; on the other hand, it must be emphasised that the best results are obtained through undetected observation, and that contact with the enemy is avoided if at all possible.

These principles are, of course, common to all armies, but in the years following the repudiation of the Versailles Treaty the *blitzkrieg* technique was being forged, and in the Panzerwaffe the requirement was for *deep* reconnaissance which could operate effectively up to 30 miles ahead of the main body.

Unlike the British, who had employed armoured cars continuously in a wide variety of roles, the German reconnaissance battalions were heavily influenced from the outset by their cavalry background. Thus their order of battle contained all the elements which were present in the cavalry screens of 1914, but reflected in the modern idiom. Instead of horses there were armoured cars; in place of foot-sore Jägers there was a motor-cycle machine-gun element; the horse artillery had been replaced by vehicle-drawn howitzers and anti-tank guns; and the assault pioneers, concerned mainly with bridging, were also mechanised.

The 1939 organisation of the Reconnaissance Battalion (Aufklärungs Abteilung or A-A) of a Panzer division consisted of a headquarters staff, two armoured reconnaissance squadrons (Panzerspähschwadronen), a motor-cycle machine-gun squadron (Kradschutzenschwadron), a heavy squadron (Schwere Schwadron), a mobile workshops, and supply and transport elements.

The battalion headquarters incorporated the usual command and control apparatus, as well as an intelligence section (Nachrichtenzug), which was responsible for correlating the information

Rear details of an SdKfz 222 belonging to Panzer-Aufklärungs-Abteilung 4 in Russia, 1943. The colour scheme appears to be yellow ochre with a serpentine overspray in green. The crew seem to be wearing the green armoured car denims, and have sand-painted helmets. The 4.Panzer-Division runes, in yellow, are visible on the right rear mudguard, balanced by a white company symbol on the left. (Bundesarchiv)

received from the squadrons and transmitting it to divisional headquarters via a troop from the divisional signals battalion.

Each armoured reconnaissance squadron consisted of a squadron headquarters containing one radio command vehicle and four armoured cars fitted with radio; one heavy troop of six six- or eight-wheeled armoured cars; and two light troops, each of six four-wheeled cars. The heavy troop could be further sub-divided into three two-car sections, and the light troops into two three-car sections, *provided* each section contained at least one car fitted with radio.

The motor-cycle machine-gun squadron employed side-car mounts and consisted of squadron headquarters, three rifle troops each of three sections armed with two MG 34s and one light mortar as integral support weapons, and one heavy troop equipped with four MG 34s.

The heavy squadron contained a number of diverse elements including a light infantry gun troop, equipped with two towed Model 18 75mm light infantry guns; a Panzerjäger troop with three (later five) towed 37mm anti-tank guns and one MG 34; and an assault pioneer troop of three sections, each armed with one MG 34.

This organisation has sometimes been described as a battle-group, but such a description is misleading. The function of the motor-cycle

Afrika Korps SdKfz 222 in desert colours with anti-grenade grilles closed. As reconnaissance troops operated in front of everyone else, it was natural that they should be wary of 'friendly fire', hence the prominent national cross on the vehicle's rear.
(RAC Tank Museum)

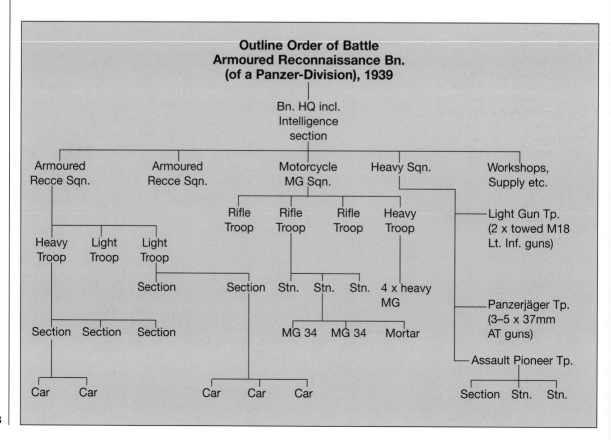

**Outline Order of Battle
Armoured Reconnaissance Bn.
(of a Panzer-Division), 1939**

Bn. HQ incl. Intelligence section

Armoured Recce Sqn. — Armoured Recce Sqn. — Motorcycle MG Sqn. — Heavy Sqn. — Workshops, Supply etc.

Heavy Troop — Light Troop — Light Troop

Rifle Troop — Rifle Troop — Rifle Troop — Heavy Troop

Section — Section — Stn. — Stn. — Stn. — 4 x heavy MG

Section — Section — Section

MG 34 — MG 34 — Mortar

Car — Car

Car — Car — Car

Light Gun Tp. (2 x towed M18 Lt. Inf. guns)

Panzerjäger Tp. (3–5 x 37mm AT guns)

Assault Pioneer Tp.

Section — Stn. — Stn.

machine-gun squadron and the weapon troops of the heavy squadron was that of shock troops, designed to case the passage of the cars through the enemy's defended zone by suppressing the opposition with a high volume of fire. Once through this zone the cars completed their mission alone. If a water obstacle lay across the route of an armoured reconnaissance squadron, part or all of the assault pioneer troop might be attached; such an attachment was far from popular with the armoured car crews, since the bridging vehicles were slow and their bulk rendered them unsuitable for use along certain routes. The armoured reconnaissance battalions of the motorised infantry divisions were similarly organised, but had only one reconnaissance squadron and lacked a heavy squadron.

At the outbreak of war the Aufklärungs-Abteilungen were deployed as follows: A-A 1 with 1st Cavalry Brigade; A-A 3, 4, 5, 7 and 8 with the Panzer divisions; A-A 2, 13, 20 and 29 with motorised infantry divisions; A-A 6 with the 1st Light Division. Somewhat larger units, Aufklärungs Regimenter 7, 8 and 9, served respectively with the 2nd, 3rd and 4th Light Divisions.

Subsequently, standardisation was achieved by adding 'armoured' to the title and by numbering or naming the Aufklärungs-Abteilungen after their parent Panzer divisions. Thus, Pz-A-A 1 served in 1. Panzer-Division, Pz-A-A 16 in 16.Panzer-Division, Pz-A-A 'GD' in the Panzer-Division 'Grossdeutschland', SS-Pz-A-A 'Totenkopf' in 3.SS-Panzer-Division 'Totenkopf', and so on. In the motorised infantry – later Panzergrenadier – divisions the Aufklärungs-Abteilungen added 100 to the number of their parent formation so that, for example, Pz-A-A 120 could readily be identified as belonging to the 20th Motorised Infantry Division. Inevitably there were exceptions to this rule, the most notable being Pz-A-A 140, which served in 22.Panzer-Division; Pz-A-A 87 of 25.Panzer-Division; and Pz-A-A 130 of the Panzer-Lehr-Division. In North Africa the official title of 21.Panzer-Division's reconnaissance battalion was Pz-A-A 200, and that of 15.Panzer-Division, Pz-A-A 15, but these units are repeatedly referred to in German accounts as A-A 3 and A-A 33 respectively.

Hitler's decision to double the number of Panzer divisions and

SdKfz 231 (6-rad) heavy armoured car in a battle-damaged village in Poland, September 1939. The large national cross on the radiator louvres, originally white, seems to have been overpainted yellow; another cross on the hull side has been completely masked. Ahead of it is a yellow W, significance unknown. (Bundesarchiv)

expand the motorised infantry branch for the invasion of Russia placed a severe strain on available resources; the reconnaissance troops were no less affected than other areas of the Panzerwaffe, many battalions entering the campaign some way short of their theoretical establishment. This, as well as the serious losses incurred not merely during the invasion itself but also in the dreadful winter that followed, made some re-organisation inevitable.

SdKfz 231 (8-rad) with barrier shield. The front and rear driving positions can he identified by the visors in the hull side. (RAC Tank Museum)

Some mention has already been made of the difficulties encountered by the four-wheeled cars during this period, the result being that their availability and importance steadily declined. Losses among motor-cycle troops generally had also been high, so serious in fact that the Panzer division's organic motor-cycle battalion was disbanded and its personnel posted to the reconnaissance battalion. This meant that the latter's organisation for a while lacked its previous tactical balance, there being somewhat too few cars and rather too many motor-cyclists.

In this interim form, the battalion's order of battle was as follows, the term 'company' having been substituted for 'squadron':

Battalion headquarters and intelligence section
One armoured car company, usually equipped with
   eight-wheeled cars
Three motor-cycle machine-gun companies
One heavy company
Mobile workshops, supply and transport

As more half-tracks became available the battalion's motor-cycle element was steadily reduced. The arrival of the 75mm 233 and later the 234/3 and various self-propelled anti-tank gun mountings, both wheeled and half-tracked, also meant that the towed weapons troops of the heavy company, always of dubious value, could be phased out. It goes almost

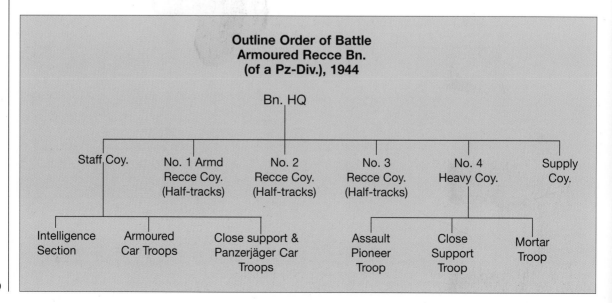

**Outline Order of Battle
Armoured Recce Bn.
(of a Pz-Div.), 1944**

Bn. HQ

| Staff Coy. | No. 1 Armd Recce Coy. (Half-tracks) | No. 2 Recce Coy. (Half-tracks) | No. 3 Recce Coy. (Half-tracks) | No. 4 Heavy Coy. | Supply Coy. |

Intelligence Section — Armoured Car Troops — Close support & Panzerjäger Car Troops

Assault Pioneer Troop — Close Support Troop — Mortar Troop

without saying that during the lengthy period of this major re-equipment no one armoured reconnaissance battalion precisely resembled another. However, by the spring of 1944 the theoretical constitution of the battalion had been tabulated as follows:

Battalion Headquarters
Staff Company (Stabskompanie)
No. 1 Armoured Reconnaissance Company (Panzerspähkompanie)
No. 2 Reconnaissance Company (Aufklärungskompanie)
No. 3 Reconnaissance Company
No. 4 Heavy Company
Supply Company (Versorgungskompanie)

The majority of these titles are misleading. The Staff Company, for example, logically incorporated the intelligence section, but also included the battalion's six armoured car troops – Radspähtrupps – which each contained three vehicles. Those four-wheeled cars still remaining were grouped into light troops, one vehicle at least being fitted with radio, but most of the troops were equipped with eight-wheelers, among which radios were now fitted as standard. A troop of three 75mm. L/24 howitzer cars also formed part of the company, joined later by a troop of Pumas or 75mm L/48 234s. The vehicles of the more heavily armed troops were allocated to other troops as their missions dictated.

The principal equipment of No. 1 Armoured Reconnaissance Company was the 250/9 reconnaissance half-track. The company was subdivided into eight three-vehicle troops – Kettenspäh-trupps – and three 250/3 radio vehicles provided rear link facilities for the company commander.

SdKfz 231 (6-rad) of Panzer-Aufklärungs-Abteilung 2 in France, June 1940. The most obvious markings on the overall Panzer grey scheme are the white outline national cross, and the 'G' identifying Guderian's XIX Panzer-Korps. just ahead of the cross are the two yellow dots used at that date by 2.Panzer-Division as a formation sign, and ahead of these the yellow-painted name 'Salzburg' in plain capitals. The log-and-hessian 'carpets' stowed on the front mudguard are for use under the rear driving wheels in bad going. This car seems to have shed its front ground-roller. The rack rigged at the top of the radiator seems to hold smoke canisters, with strings led back through the driver's visor – an improvisation entirely in keeping with the reconnaissance role in a campaign involving deep penetration of enemy lines. (Bundesarchiv)

Nos. 2 and 3 Reconnaissance Companies were also equipped with the 250 half-track series. Each consisted of a company headquarters, three reconnaissance troops and a heavy weapons troop. The headquarters section included two 250/3 rear-link radio vehicles, and each reconnaissance troop contained seven 250/1 armoured personnel carriers, subdivided into one troop headquarters vehicle and three sections of two vehicles each. The heavy weapons troop consisted of one 250/1 in troop headquarters; a close support section of two 250/8 self-propelled 75mm L/24 howitzers and one 250/1 APC; and a mortar section of two 250/7 80mm mortar carriers and one 250/1 APC.

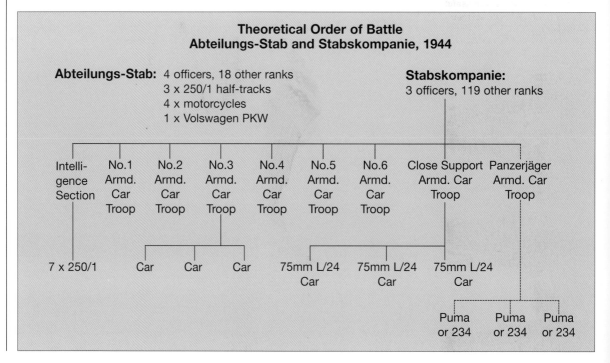

Abandoned SdKfz 250/2 telephone vehicle, North Africa. The marking below the Afrika Korps palm indicates that it belonged to a towed howitzer battery. (RAC Tank Museum)

The conception of the half-tracked reconnaissance company was not simply that of a replacement for the old motor-cycle machine-gun squadron, although it did incorporate its role, which it was able to perform with ease since its establishment provided for no less than 48 machine-guns as well as the organic heavy weapons support mentioned above. Fully equipped with radio, its primary task was reconnaissance; its

Theoretical Order of Battle
Abteilungs-Stab and Stabskompanie, 1944

Abteilungs-Stab: 4 officers, 18 other ranks
3 x 250/1 half-tracks
4 x motorcycles
1 x Volswagen PKW

Stabskompanie:
3 officers, 119 other ranks

Intelligence Section	No.1 Armd. Car Troop	No.2 Armd. Car Troop	No.3 Armd. Car Troop	No.4 Armd. Car Troop	No.5 Armd. Car Troop	No.6 Armd. Car Troop	Close Support Armd. Car Troop	Panzerjäger Armd. Car Troop
7 x 250/1	Car	Car	Car	75mm L/24 Car	75mm L/24 Car	75mm L/24 Car		
							Puma or 234	Puma or 234	Puma or 234

provision of Panzergrenadier support for armoured car or armoured reconnaissance company operations had now become a secondary rôle, invoked at the battalion commander's discretion.

No. 4 Heavy Company consisted of an assault pioneer troop, a close support troop and a mortar troop. The assault pioneers, in addition to their bridge repair role, were also responsible for demolition; this included the removal of barriers if the battalion was leading an advance and the destruction of bridges if it was covering a withdrawal. They were also specialists in certain combat techniques, and their order of battle included a section of six man-pack flamethrowers. The troop's theoretical establishment was seven SdKfz 251/5s, the assault pioneer version of the medium half-track, but whether these were available in sufficient numbers is doubtful, and suitably modified 250/Is would have taken their place. The close support troop nominally consisted of six 251/9 self-propelled 75mm L/24 howitzers, and the mortar troop of six 251/2 80mm mortar carriers, but in practice the 250/8 and 250/7 were frequently used.

This battalion organisation, like others of the period, represents what was desirable rather than attainable. The majority of reconnaissance battalions were below strength during the last year of the war, and expedience and improvisation were the order of the day, commanding officers using whatever equipment they could obtain to carry out their missions.

Something of the method adopted by German reconnaissance units is described by Oberst a.D. Fabian von Bonin von Ostau, who served in Panzer-Aufklärungs-Abteilung 1: 'Having been given a task by division, the commanding officer would despatch several troops along the most important axes and lead them personally. Behind him, the squadron thickened up the screen with further troops. As an officer commanding a section of two eight-wheeled cars, I carried out tasks given to me directly by the commanding officer. I was given a distant objective, perhaps 20 to 40 kilometres into enemy territory, and, without consideration of neighbouring recce sections, had to reach this using my own initiative. Enemy forces had to be reported and if possible circumvented without detection so that we could penetrate deep into their rear areas. Often we had not reached our objective by nightfall and remained as stationary observers, on suitable features, until daybreak. On reaching the objective we were either ordered to return to our unit or were relieved by another recce section that had followed us up. Occasionally we

A pair of SdKfz 232 Schwere Panzerspähwagen (6-rad) (Fu) entering Prague during the German takeover. Details of the rear driving visors are clearly visible; and to the left of them what appears to be a tiny white cross marking. The rear driver of the right hand vehicle is raising his domed hatch to peer out. The invasions of Austria and Czechoslovakia provided the Panzerwaffe as a whole with useful 'dry runs' in which to perfect their techniques.

remained stationary in enemy territory until such time as our own division caught up with us.

'At first one had to overcome and become used to a feeling of loneliness, of being all alone in enemy territory without being able to rely on outside help. With increasing experience, one's self-confidence grew; apart from which, such independent missions were particularly attractive to a young cavalry officer in that one was not pressed into a restrictive framework with one's superiors and neighbours.

'The initial penetration into unknown enemy territory was difficult. For this purpose our own local attacks were taken advantage of before the enemy could recover his balance. When one had achieved some penetration, the advance became easier. A recce leader must be a good observer and have a nose for knowing where he might run into the enemy. Mostly the cars were well camouflaged and used all available natural cover, following each other with the last car covering the rear. On features where a good field of vision was offered, one halted and made a thorough observation. If no enemy were seen then the first car went on to the next observation point under surveillance, when it arrived safely the next car was called forward.

SdKfz 232 Schwere Panzerspähwagen (8-rad) (Fu) in mint condition. The photo clearly illustrates the working of the swivel aerial mounting which permitted the turret all-round traverse. (Bundesarchiv)

'It was important to make a thorough observation of villages as these were nearly always used by the enemy in one form or another. If you see the enemy, then you know. If the enemy is not visible and the civilian population is going about its normal business, then the village is not enemy occupied. If no people are seen, this is highly suspicious and the village should be by-passed by a wide margin.

'The best patrols I had were those with clean guns. Even worthwhile targets were only reported and not engaged; that is the business of others. A troop leader with a tendency to bang away is useless for reconnaissance purposes since he is soon located by the enemy and chased like a rabbit. A report giving the location of an enemy tank leaguer is of infinitely more value than five shot-up lorries.

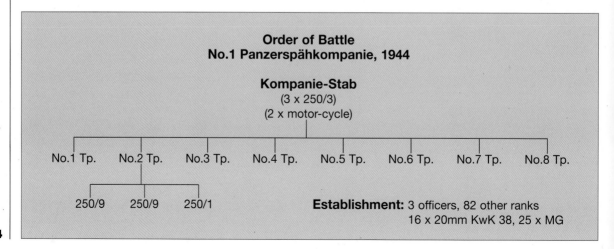

Order of Battle
No.1 Panzerspähkompanie, 1944

Kompanie-Stab
(3 x 250/3)
(2 x motor-cycle)

No.1 Tp. No.2 Tp. No.3 Tp. No.4 Tp. No.5 Tp. No.6 Tp. No.7 Tp. No.8 Tp.

250/9   250/9   250/1

Establishment: 3 officers, 82 other ranks
16 x 20mm KwK 38, 25 x MG

1. **SdKfz 232 Schwere Panzerspähwagen (6-rad) (Fu), unit unknown; Army manoeuvres, Germany 1937 or 1938**

2. **SdKfz 13 Scout Car, unit unknown, Poland, 1939**

A

1. SdKfz 222 Panzerspähwagen,
SS-Panzer Aufklärungs Abteilung
'Leibstandarte Adolf Hitler'; Greece, 1941

2. SdKfz 232 Schwere Panzerspähwagen (8-rad),
SS-Panzer Aufklärungs Abteilung
'Leibstandarte Adolf Hitler'; Greece, 1941

B

1. SdKfz 222 Panzerspähwagen,
   5. Leichte-Division, DAK; Libya, 1941

2. SdKfz 263 Command Car (8-rad),
   5. Leichte-Division, DAK; Libya, 1941

SCHWERE PANZERSPÄHWAGEN SdKfz 234/4

1   V-12 cylinder air-cooled Tatra 103 diesel motor 200 PS at 2250rpm
2   Diesel injectors
3   Silencer left hand side
4   Intake fans for air-cooled engine
5   Rear armour 10mm
6   Rear inspection hatch
7   Smoke bottle holders
8   Exhaust pipe armoured cover
9   Silencer right hand side
10 Axe
11 Pick
12 Rear tool bin
13 Main stowage bin
14 8 wheel drive and steering
15 Tyres size 270/20
16 Rear driving steering wheel
17 Independent suspension swing arms and drive shaft
18 Rear driver's seat
19 Platform for mounting machine-gun
20 Right hand side ammunition bin, 12 rounds
21 Fire extinguisher
22 Wire cutter
23 Front tool bin
24 Signal pistol ammunition container
25 Gear shift lever
26 Horizontal sliding breech
27 Cut out in roof to accommodate traverse of gun when depressed
28 Forward driver position with inverted steering wheel
29 Vehicle width guides
30 Front armour 30mm
31 Side armoured vision port
32 Instrument panel
33 Drivers escape hatch in 15mm glasis armour
34 Driver armoured vision port
35 Travel lock for gun
36 7.92mm MG 42 machine-gun
37 7.5cm PaK 40 L/46 anti-tank gun
38 Muzzlebrake
39 2 x 4mm spaced armour gun shield
40 Breech cocking spring
41 Recoil guard
42 2 metre rod antenna for radio
43 Rear gear shift lever
44 Rack for fire extinguisher
45 Recoil guide
46 Crew side escape hatch (sealed on the SdKfz 234/4)
47 Extra armoured superstructure (14.5mm) for SdKfz 234/4
48 Jack
49 Side armour 8mm
50 Cooling air outlet grill
51 Air Intake cleaner
52 Air intake grill
53 Engine inspection hatch
54 Fuel cans
55 Motor cover armour 5.5mm

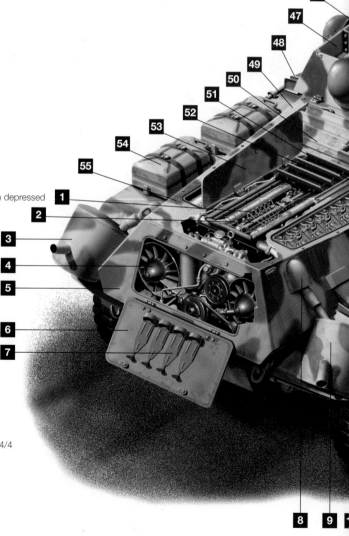

D

SPECIFICATIONS

Crew: 4
Combat weight: 11,500kg
Motor: 12 cylinder Tatra 103 13.8 liter
  air-cooled diesel 200 metric horse power
  at 2250rpm
Power-to-weight ratio: 17.39 metric
HP/Ton
Overall length: 6,000mm
Width: 2,400mm
Transmission: 6 forward, 6 reverse
Steering: 8 wheel steering and drive
Maximum speed (road): 80kmph

Maximum speed (cross country): 30kmph
Fording: 1,200mm
Maximum range: 900km at cruising speed
Armament: 7.5cm PaK 40L/46
Elevation: -3 to +22 degrees
Traverse: 12 degrees right 12 degrees left
Main gun: 7.5cm Pzgr. 39 *(Armour piercing)*
Ammunition: 7.5cm Pzgr. 40 *(AP -
Tungsten core)*
  7.5 cm Sprgr. 34 *(High explosive)*
Sight: Zielfehrnrohr 3 x 8 *(Monocular)*
Stowed main gun rounds: 24

1. SdKfz 250/3 radio half-track 'Greif' used by Rommel as a command vehicle during his capture of Tobruk, June 1942

2. SdKfz 261 Kleiner Panzerfunkwagen, unit unknown, Panzerarmee Afrika; Libya, 1941

1. SdKfz 250/10
   Self-propelled 37mm Anti-tank Gun,
   Pz-A-A 'Grossdeutschland'; Russia, spring 1943

2. SdKfz 221 Panzerspähwagen,
   unit unknown; Russia,
   winter 1941–1942

F

**1. SdKfz 250/3 radio half-track,
unit unknown, Panzergruppe von Kleist;
South Russia, late summer 1943**

**2. SdKfz 232 Schwere
Panzerspähwagen (8-rad),
Pz-A-A 115; Italy, 1944**

Clearly-marked SdKfz 232 (8-rad) (Fu) of the 1st Armoured Reconnaissance Sqn., Panzer-Aufklärungs-Abteilung 'Grossdeutschland' in rail transit near Kursk, June 1942. The turrets have been sheeted down, and each bears the Reichsbahn's shipping label. The leading car has been fitted with a frontal shield with which to force its way through barriers. The slight right-hand lock illustrates perfectly the effect of eight-wheel steering. (Bundesarchiv)

'Reports were made in Morse and communications were good.[1] The operators were well trained and could send reports quickly, but it was up to the section commander to formulate the report. This soon became a matter of routine. Voice transmissions were used only between vehicles. Every report concerning the enemy's whereabouts, and even negative information contained in periodic situation reports, helped build up a picture of the overall enemy situation.

'The essential ingredients of a successful reconnaissance section were a well drilled team, mutual confidence and strong nerves. Our main thought was always "There is always a way out and all is not lost so long as one is alive."

'Once our invasion of Russia had been halted in December 1941, fresh Siberian formations were pitched against troops who had no experience of winter warfare conditions. The Army had to fight a series of delaying actions until a defence line could be established on the Upper Volga. During this period the reconnaissance battalions performed vital work as covering forces, concealing from the enemy the details of our own movements and intentions. For this purpose the armoured reconnaissance squadrons, with their good communications equipment, were deployed over a wide area under their squadron leaders. In defence, the fighting element of the battalion, that is the motor-cycle troops and the heavy company, were deployed mainly in the front line, while the armoured car troops were given specific missions by Division.'

When covering a withdrawal the method employed by the reconnaissance battalions was the reverse of that used in the advance. The armoured reconnaissance squadrons remained in concealed observation positions after their division had disengaged, while the remainder of the battalion established temporary defensive fronts, usually based on narrow-frontage features such as a bridge or causeway, through which the cars would withdraw when they received the order to retire. In these circumstances the two major tasks of the armoured reconnaissance squadrons were to screen the divisional flanks and rearguard against observation by the enemy's reconnaissance units, and to report on the enemy thrust lines as they developed. From the flow of information provided by the cars, the divisional commander was able to adjust his plans according to the needs of the moment and so conclude the successful extraction of his command. The cars were recalled when the division had consolidated its main defence line and would retire

---

[1] Transmissions using carrier wave, i.e. Morse, had a greater range than those using voice.

through their own battalion's interim defence lines while bridges were blown up, trees felled and roads mined behind them.

Notwithstanding the use of all possible means to achieve its ends by stealth, deception and concealment, armoured reconnaissance was – and remains – an extremely dangerous game, and the average troop leader had an active, testing, but all too frequently short career. Oberst von Bonin von Ostau was wounded on three separate occasions, and of four of his fellow troop leaders who joined at the same time, three were killed during the 1941–1942 fighting and the fourth the following year.

An SdKfz 232 (8-rad) (Fu) leads the way through a ruined Greek village, spring 1941. Some attempt seems to have been made to overpaint the original 'Panzer grey' scheme with a light (sand?) shade, but much of this has worn off, and the barrier shield has not been repainted at all. The name 'Seydlitz' appears on the hull side in white Gothic script. The second vehicle is an SdKfz 221 light armoured car, mounting a smaller turret than the 222. (Bundesarchiv)

ARMOURED RECONNAISSANCE IN ACTION

The history of the German armoured reconnaissance battalions contains numerous examples of ambush, hard-fought running battles and hair-raising escapes; but while it is tempting to stray into this area, it must be remembered that such actions usually took place because something had gone badly wrong. It is, therefore, of greater benefit to examine the

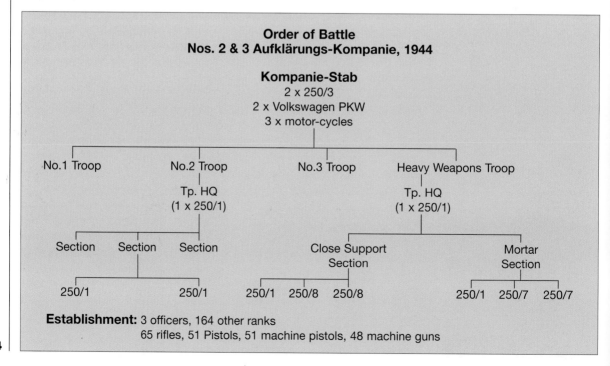

Order of Battle
Nos. 2 & 3 Aufklärungs-Kompanie, 1944

Kompanie-Stab
2 x 250/3
2 x Volkswagen PKW
3 x motor-cycles

No.1 Troop   No.2 Troop   No.3 Troop   Heavy Weapons Troop

No.2 Troop — Tp. HQ (1 x 250/1)
Heavy Weapons Troop — Tp. HQ (1 x 250/1)

Section   Section   Section   Close Support Section   Mortar Section

250/1   250/1   250/1   250/8   250/8   250/1   250/7   250/7

Establishment: 3 officers, 164 other ranks
65 rifles, 51 Pistols, 51 machine pistols, 48 machine guns

activities of a patrol which achieved its purpose. and the following account, written by Oberst Hans Freiherr von Esebeck for the *Berliner Illustrierte Zeitung*, in 1941, describes the opening of Wavell's Operation 'Battleaxe' from the viewpoint of the German reconnaissance troops:

'The locality is in no respect worthy of mention. The landscape stretches away endlessly, a sand-desert covered with scanty, dried-up camel scrub. At the Egyptian frontier the total desert begins. At noon, when the wind blows from the south, the dust swoops along in dense spirals. There is nothing, absolutely nothing, to break the monotony of this desolate expanse.

'The three armoured cars are now pounding at high speed through the wire fence that divides Libya from Egypt. It is broken in many places, scarcely a barrier any longer. The war has scarred it and the wind has cluttered it with paper and rubbish carried from afar. The sand is knee-deep, being constantly carried away and heaped up afresh. Day in and day out, a breeze sweeps across the level expanse.

'Oberfeldwebel Barlesius can now see the armoured cars he is to relieve. In the dusk they look like strange black monsters. Their position is marked on the map, and they have been found by accurate use of the compass. This is the only way of finding patrols stationed near the enemy in the area south of Sollum and Capuzzo.

'A boring business! During the day one observes, as far as any observation is possible in the shimmering haze. At night, one depends upon one's hearing. If the wind is right, it carries voices with it. Sometimes one can hear a jackal or the barking of a desert fox; sometimes the distant creaking of the tracks of a British tank; and sometimes a strange bird-call. The nights are refreshingly cold. During the day the sun beats down on men and vehicles from a cloudless sky. The plates of the vehicles become red hot. Anyone who is careless will be showing the doctor a burnt hand the following day. Some practice is required before one can climb into a car without touching the metal or

An SdKfz 250/3 command vehicle on the move with a Panzergrenadier battlegroup including several of its larger SdKfz 251 cousins and a PzKpfw II. Russia, 1942. (US National Archives)

brushing against it with one's bare legs. In the morning they spread out canvas from the car and support it with two poles to provide a little shade. The flies are bad. As far as the eyes can see, nothing but sand and stones; and yet flies live in the desert. There is no relief from them. Barlesius fills a tin with camel dung, pours petrol on top and then adds some water to the rising flames. Dense, biting smoke drifts upwards. The

SdKfz 232 (8-rad) (Fu) on internal security duty in a Cretan village, 1943 – not very arduous duty, apparently. Note the simple pole aerial replacing the frame array. (Martin Windrow)

flies vanish but in half an hour they are back again. There is only one effective remedy which nature herself supplies in the form of a sandstorm. During these the heat is stifling but one must protect oneself with goggles and a cloth wrapped around the nose, mouth and ears, or the fine dust will penetrate every pore.

'No one need envy the patrols. Somewhere a name is written on the map. It is printed in black in the middle of an area of white. A *bir* lies here, a dry well of immense antiquity, deep in the rocky earth. Or a couple of heaps of stones bear witness to a long departed life. All around stretches the limitless desert. Nothing stirs in any direction. The hollows and wadis which repeatedly intersect the plain are invisible in the sunlight. In the morning and in the evening when the air becomes clear the armoured cars drive a few kilometres forward. Cautiously they make their way forward and sometimes they encounter their opposite numbers. Both sides observe each other through glasses. Now and then they exchange loud and unfriendly greetings, turn about and retire to their regular positions. It is

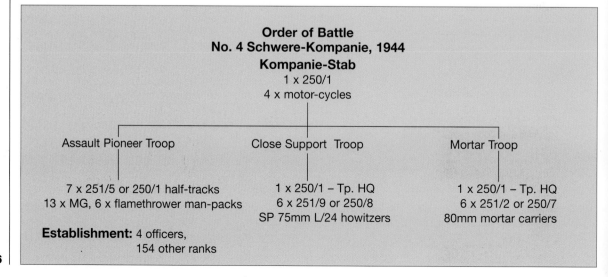

Order of Battle
No. 4 Schwere-Kompanie, 1944
Kompanie-Stab
1 x 250/1
4 x motor-cycles

Assault Pioneer Troop	Close Support Troop	Mortar Troop
7 x 251/5 or 250/1 half-tracks	1 x 250/1 – Tp. HQ	1 x 250/1 – Tp. HQ
13 x MG, 6 x flamethrower man-packs	6 x 251/9 or 250/8 SP 75mm L/24 howitzers	6 x 251/2 or 250/7 80mm mortar carriers

Establishment: 4 officers, 154 other ranks

doubtless an important business, but certainly a boring and a soul-destroying one.

'Barlesius has now reached the three armoured cars he is to relieve. Greetings are exchanged. "Always the same thing – nothing doing" says their commander. "This morning three British tanks appeared about two kilometres away, but they've gone now."

'"New faces?" "Our old friends at Point 193. Have you brought any mail?" Barlesius nods. A bundle is handed out. Mail – the most important word in Africa! The men gather round, collecting their letters and newspapers, then go with long strides to their vehicles. They read quickly before starting off.

'"Communications with unit established!" announces the radio operator. "Good. State the time – the others are leaving."

'Wilde is today at Point 204, Peglow at Sidi Omar, and this place is Sidi Suliman. Heaven only knows how this ancient heap of stones came by its high-sounding name. Barlesius remembers how the first time he visited Point 204 he could not find it, because only when you get there do you realise that it does give an extensive view – provided the sun does not bewitch the whole desolate waste.

'"Coffee, Oberfeldwebel!" "Thanks." It is certainly not Mokka, but it is wet and cool. In the last silvery light of the day the land stands out clearly once more. Then, without transition, the light is extinguished by night. The crews sit round in a circle eating their *alter Mann* [old man], that tinned meat with the printed inscription "A.M." from which it gets the nickname that the African soldier will remember to his dying day. The water bottle containing cold coffee is held to the lips. Very welcome after a journey during which there is always plenty of dust to swallow. They talk a little before turning in. It is a warm night. Only one blanket is needed and the tent canvas for the morning dew.

'About one o'clock Barlesius is awakened by someone shaking him. It is Schneider. "There's something wrong, sir. There is a continuous roar of engines."

'Barlesius is awake in an instant. People are stirring around the other cars. The silhouettes of the soldiers stand out against the sky. All listen intently. There! They hear it quite plainly. The distant roar of engines; like the drone of bumblebees. "They're a long way off." Barlesius jumps to the ground and kneels with his ear close to the earth. There can be no doubt about it. "Michel, start up! Bearing 43!"

'Barlesius swings himself onto the car which starts up noiselessly. "Halt after two kilometres – and keep a sharp look-out!" The darkness swallows them up. Compass in hand, the Oberfeldwebel tries in vain to pierce the surrounding blackness. They hear it more plainly now – a low

Nice study of an SdKfz 233 (8-rad) 75mm captured in N. Africa in almost new condition. The only marking on the neat sand-coloured overspray is the numberplate. (RAC Tank Museum)

rumble mingled with a high squeaking. "Cars – about!" It is 0130 hours when the first radio message goes out: "Loud noise of engines from south and south-east. Ten kilometres distant."

'Not far from Capuzzo, in a *bir*, lies the battalion's headquarters. The huge rock cave in which a constant, pleasant temperature prevails is organised as a battle headquarters. In the first rocky vault are housed the orderlies and wireless operators. In the passage to the second chamber the commander sleeps. The adjutant is now standing before him. A candle throws bizarre shadows on the grey walls.

'"Message from Barlesius, sir." The major, drunk with sleep, reaches for the paper. "Nothing else? Then we'll wait. I think the others will come up if anything happens."

'At 0215 a transmission is received from Wilde – "Loud sound of engines from the south-east."

'"Well, well!" The commander is now wide awake. "Inform Division. Ask whether they have received any other messages. Perhaps Halfaya have been on. If so, we know what we are about!"

'The orderly pours water into the English petrol tin. The major plunges his head in. The soap does not lather. The water is salty as always. You can taste it in the tea. It is 0300 hours when Barlesius comes on the air again: "Sound of engines coming nearer. Probably tracked vehicles." The Commander merely nods. "It's about time. Mark my words, Tommy has intentions on Halfaya – revenge for the 27th May. It's been long enough in coming." [1]

'At 0440 hours Barlesius transmits another signal: "Enemy tanks from the south and south-east. Am retiring northwards!" The German front has long since awakened. At Division, General Rommel too has slid out of bed with a "Well, well!"

'It has slowly grown light. The air becomes clear, almost transparent. In the grey light of dawn visibility is good and Barlesius recognises the grey monsters plainly through his glasses. From all sides they are making for the north-west and north, raising clouds of dust. "The tracks are

---

[1] 27 May 1941 was the date Rommel re-captured Halfaya Pass, which had been lost during Operation 'Brevity'.

Reconnaissance troops regularly worked with the artillery's Forward Observation Officers. The vehicle shown here, photographed during the 1940 campaign in France, is the SdKfz 251/18 artillery observation half-track. The tactical markings are those of 1.Panzer-Division and No. 7 Company 1st Motor Rifle Regiment, suggesting that the latter have been required to surrender it to the FOO. The superstructure has been modified to provide a broad, flat surface for the FOO's maps and artillery board. The column is overtaking one of the few assault gun batteries to have fought in France at this time. (US National Archives)

armoured, Oberfeldwebel!" This Barlesius has already noticed. Thick plates over the tracks mean Matildas, contraptions with 80mm armour plating; not easy nuts to crack. "It is time." Barlesius raises his hand. Engines jump to life and the fast and manoeuvrable reconnaissance cars move off. "Direction – Point 206!"

'At 0500 they meet Wilde's patrol. Barlesius radios once again: "Ten enemy tanks four kilometres south of 206!" [At this point the armoured cars were joined by a Panzerjäger unit which inflicted some loss on the Matilda squadron and then withdrew, heavily outnumbered. A full account of this action is contained in Vanguard No. 12, *Sturmartillerie and Panzerjäger.*]

'Barlesius does not remain idle during this encounter. He continues to reconnoitre, slipping by the enemy at 400 metres and continuing to report the details of his advance. More and more enemy tanks appear. Quite a number have gone by to the right and left of Point 206. The Panzerjägers and the motor-cycle troops, who have appeared from nowhere, have already disengaged and withdrawn. For Barlesius there is only a slim chance that he will get back unscathed, but he has to take it. After brief reflection he simply drives past under the noses of the tanks. They fire furiously. Their shots crack past the three cars but they come through unharmed and eventually rejoin their unit. Oberfeldwebel Barlesius has opened the great battle.'[1]

The early warning provided by the German armoured car outposts lost Wavell's troops any element of surprise, and the Axis forces were fully prepared for their attack. Heavy losses incurred during the opening phase, followed by muddle and misunderstanding, all contributed to a

---

[1] For those readers interested in uniform history, a colour plate based on a photo of Ofw. Barlesius of A-A 33 is found in Men-at-Arms 24 (revised) *The Panzer Divisions*

British reverse that was to cost Wavell and other senior officers their appointments.

Even so, one would hesitate in describing Operation 'Battleaxe' as a great battle, although the German reaction to their success is entirely understandable. Notwithstanding, the article does convey the essence of the reconnaissance soldier's lifestyle; long periods of isolation, boredom, discomfort and incessant watchfulness, followed by short, sharp periods of intense and terrifying activity. It shows, too, the paramount importance of good communications, the need for brief, clear and accurate transmissions, and the cautious evaluation of contact reports by battalion headquarters. Above all, it demonstrates the truth of the old saying that the reconnaissance troops are the eyes and ears of the army. Without them, any commander is left blind and groping in the fog of war.

The SdKfz 234/4 Panzerspähwagen 75mm PAK 40 L/48, as displayed at the RAC Tank Museum, Bovington. The mudguards and side stowage bins have been removed to reveal the suspension details and the monocoque construction of the hull. The armoured superstructure masks the rear driver's side visors. (RAC Tank Museum)

Other roles

While it has been emphasised that the primary role of armoured reconnaissance units was to obtain information, preferably without having to fight for it, their overall operational perspective underwent a change during the second half of the war. By then, Germany had been thrown onto the strategic defensive and there was therefore less need for the deep reconnaissance necessary in major offensive operations. Instead, on the Eastern Front particularly, where commanders with limited resources were forced to form ad hoc battlegroups with whatever troops they could lay their hands on, armoured reconnaissance units found themselves increasingly drawn into combat operations. In Italy, too, where the terrain was unsuited to mechanised operations, they sometimes found themselves manning a sector of the line, while in the West, where Allied air power controlled the skies, their activities were even further curtailed, save in unusual circumstances. Three brief examples will suffice.

In January 1943 German fortunes in Russia were at one of their lowest ebbs. The Sixth Army and part of the Fourth Panzer Army had been isolated in Stalingrad and the priority had become to hold open a corridor through which Army Group A could withdraw from the Caucasus, thereby escaping the possibility of a similar encirclement.

One of the formations engaged in holding open the corridor was 11th Panzer Division, commanded by Major-general Hermann Balck, a master of mechanized warfare at the tactical and operational levels. During the fourth week of January the Russians established a bridgehead at Manutchskaya, a village located at the confluence of the rivers Manich and Don, only 20 miles from Rostov, through which most of the troops from the Caucasus were streaming. Elimination of the bridgehead was therefore essential, but a probe on the 24th revealed that the enemy had dug in and concealed their tanks among the houses in the southern half of the village, where they were difficult to spot and deal with. Balck decided to flush them out the following day with a simulated tank attack on their northern perimeter, using his reconnaissance unit's armoured cars and half-tracks covered by a smoke screen. This had the desired effect and, once the Russian tanks were moving, the divisional artillery, less one battery detailed to maintain the smoke screen, concentrated its fire on a pre-selected break-in point at the southern edge of the village. Through this burst the division's Panzer regiment, destroying its opponents in a sharp fight among the houses. The remaining defenders fled but were pursued by Panzergrenadiers and shot down. Russian losses exceeded 500 men, plus 20 tanks destroyed; German casualties amounted to one man killed and fourteen wounded.

On 9 September 1943 the Western Allies effected a landing in the Gulf of Salerno on the west coast of Italy. Closest to the landing site was 16.Panzer-Division, which had come close to destruction during the Stalingrad fighting but, having refitted in France, was once again at full strength. While the rest of the division moved forward to contain the beachhead, Pz-A-A 16 set up observation posts on the high ground overlooking the gulf and monitored the progress of the landing, sending back a stream of reports that enabled the German commanders to

An extremely interesting photo showing German troops during the final phase of a disengagement on the Eastern Front. The destruction of the village not only produces a smoke screen to cover the operation, but also prevents its use by the Red Army. The 37mm anti-tank gun team are manhandling their weapon towards its towing vehicle, covered by the armoured car, which will be 'last away'. The car is a captured Russian BA-10, of which several variants existed; in general, few Russian cars were taken into German service. This example is marked with a German national cross and the name 'Jaguar' in Gothic script. (Martin Windrow)

co-ordinate their response. Its task was complicated by the fact that the surrender of Italy coincided with the landing, but due allowance had been made for this and once the appropriate codeword was, received some of the battalion's strength was diverted to disarm the nearest Italian units; this was accomplished without serious incident, most of its erstwhile allies being only to glad of the opportunity to change into civilian clothes and make their way home. Naval gunfire eventually forced the reconnaissance teams to abandon their observation posts and drive inland, but even here they had a role to play, rounding up numerous stragglers from a scattered American air drop. All in all, Pz-A-A 16 made a most useful contribution to the German containment of the beachhead during the critical early stages of what became a very bitter battle indeed.

The larger SdKfz 251/4 artillery tractor was used to tow the 75mm liG (light infantry gun) M18 which equipped the armoured reconnaissance battalions' Light Gun Troops. (US National Archives)

Nevertheless, employment of armoured reconnaissance battalions in the combat role was by no means universally successful. At Arnhem a year later the northern end of the road bridge was captured by 2nd Battalion The Parachute Regiment and elements of other units under the overall command of Lieutenant-colonel John Frost. The effect of this was to disrupt the operations of II SS Panzer Korps, which was simultaneously engaged with substantial Allied forces at Nijmegen, to the south. After dusk on the evening of 17 September a rash attempt was made to clear the bridge with a counter-attack from the south, using infantry in four unarmoured lorries. As Frost's men occupied the upper storeys of buildings overlooking the northern ramp, the result was a foregone conclusion. The riddled lorries careered to standstill near a blazing hut and soon began to burn themselves. There was little fight left in their surviving occupants who quickly gave up.

Recapturing the bridge now became a matter of the utmost importance. While Frost's perimeter came under sustained attack from the north, east and west, a further attempt was made to storm the bridge from the south on the morning of 18 September, spearheaded by SS-Hauptsturmführer Paul Graber's SS-Pz-A-A 9 (9.SS-Panzer-Division 'Hohenstaufen'). At 09:30 five armoured cars tore on to the bridge with guns blazing. Expertly handled, they swerved past the still-smouldering lorries and, avoiding all but one of the Teller mines placed in the road by the paratroopers, tore down the northern ramp into the town where, for the moment, they took no further part in the engagement. In their wake came the main assault, consisting of half-tracks and more armoured cars, infantry in lorries protected by grain sacks, then more infantry on foot, firing as they came. By now, the paratroopers had

overcome their initial surprise and, as soon as the leading vehicles were level with the houses overlooking the ramp, they opened fire with every weapon at their disposal, including anti-tank guns, PIATs, automatic weapons, rifles and grenades. The two leading half-tracks ground to a standstill with all aboard them dead. The wounded driver of the third vehicle, seized by panic, reversed at speed into the oncoming half-track behind. Locked together, the two vehicles careered across the carriageway and caught fire. The rest of the column tried to batter its way through but only added to the growing tangle. One or two vehicles, out of control, smashed through the ramp wall and crashed to the road below. Pinned down amid the wreckage, the attackers tried to fight on. The paratroopers' mortar platoon joined in the carnage, followed by 1st Airborne Division's 75mm pack howitzers, firing from Oosterbeek under the direction of an FOO at the bridge. Two hours after their attack had begun, the SS men broke and fled, pursued by derisive yells from the paratroopers. For all practical purposes, SS-Pz-A-A 9 had been wiped out; its commander, who had led the attack with suicidal courage, now lay dead on the bridge.

ABOVE AND BELOW RIGHT
The end of SS-Pz-A-A 9. Two aerial views showing the wreckage of this battalion's armoured cars, half-tracks and other vehicles at the northern end of Arnhem road bridge following its abortive attack on 18 September 1944. (Imperial War Museum)

THE PLATES

A1. SdKfz 232 Schwere Panzerspähwagen (6-rad) (Fu), unit unknown; Army manoeuvres, Germany, 1937 or 1938

This vehicle was the radio version of the standard six-wheeled heavy armoured car – SdKfz 231 (6-rad). Our painting shows clearly the method of attaching the heavy 'bedstead' aerial to the car – namely two fixed brackets at the rear of the hull and a rotating central pivot from which arms descended to the turret, thus permitting all-round traverse. The vehicle is finished in Panzer grey with the irregular brown overspray seen in 1935–1939 and is unmarked, although the red and white pennant suggests a command car in a unit operating directly under Army command. This may well explain the slightly smug expression of the Feldgendarme, or 'Chain Dog' as he was more popularly known, who seems to be enjoying the delay he is imposing on a very senior crew!

A2. SdKfz 13 Scout Car, unit unknown, Poland 1939

Known for obvious reasons as 'The Bathtub', this vehicle had entered service with the cavalry in 1933, but by the start of the Second World War had been relegated to the heavy company of the infantry divisions' reconnaissance battalions. This example is finished overall in Panzer grey, with the prominent white national cross employed during the Polish campaign. Also in white is the Aufklärungskompanie symbol on mudguard (see inset), and above this can be seen a skeleton-frame for a command pennant. The number plate seems to have been plastered with mud, perhaps not intentionally, but the headlights have been masked to prevent reflected glare.

A dramatic Eastern Front photograph showing an SdKfz 250/1 reconnaissance troop driving past a field of fiercely burning crops. (RAC Tank Museum)

B1. SdKfz 222 Panzerspähwagen, SS-Panzer Aufklärungs Abteilung 'Leibstandarte Adolf Hitler'; Greece, 1941

The car is finished in Panzer grey, but has been overlaid with a heavy coating of pale dust. Towards the rear of the vehicle can be seen the LSSAH unit sign of a shield and skeleton key in white, while below the turret in black Gothic lettering is the name 'Walter Schultz', almost certainly to commemorate a fallen comrade. External stowage includes a washbowl and a bedroll, while ingenious use has been made of a camouflage net to stow various other items of personal equipment on the front of the vehicle. Inset is the tactical symbol of the 1st Troop of the battalion's motor-cycle machine-gun squadron.

B2. SdKfz 232 Schwere Panzerspähwagen (8-rad), SS-Panzer Aufklärungs Abteilung 'Leibstandarte Adolf Hitler'; Greece, 1941

The plain grey finish of this car is relieved only by the black-outlined-white national cross and by a white tactical marking showing that the car belongs to the battalion's 2nd armoured reconnaissance squadron – note also the white-outlined-black SS number plate. The space behind the forward shield has been used for stowage, including that of a rather battered briefcase, an appendage as popular in Germany as the bowler hat in England. Inset are details of the squadron tactical marking and the marking carried by the battalion's staff signals section.

C1. SdKfz 222 Panzerspähwagen, 5.Leichte-Division, DAK; Libya, 1941

The harsh effect of blowing sand has eroded the sand-coloured overspray to such an extent that the original Panzer grey colour scheme is starting to show through, particularly on the turret. At the rear of the vehicle a small area has been left unsprayed, and in this is a white outline national cross. The vehicle interior retains its original grey, as is apparent from the open side hatch. The skeleton command pennant bracket suggests that the car served with divisional headquarters.

Desert outpost, of the kind manned by Ofw. Barlesius and his men of A-A 33. The vehicles are four SdKfz 222s and a single 232 (8-rad) (Fu). The landscape conveys well the monotonous immensity of their task. (Bundesarchiv)

Autumn 1942: SdKfz 253 half-track engaged in street fighting around Leningrad. This 'Leichter Gepanzerter Beobachtungs-kraftwagen' version had a partially roofed-in hull – note split round hatch used by MG 34 gunner. The potential for close-quarter action is hinted by the MP 40 and the Russian PPSh41 sub-machine-guns lying within easy reach of the crew. (Martin Windrow)

C2. SdKfz 263 Command Car (8-rad), 5.Leichte-Division, DAK; Libya, 1941

Once again, the sand overspray has been eroded to such an extent that the original grey colour scheme is showing through. Two areas have been deliberately left grey for marking purposes: one, forward, contains the Afrika Korps palm in white, and the other, aft, the insignia of 3.Panzer-Division, the vehicle's original owners, also in white. The

Deception takes many forms, but this is surely one of the most unusual! Few enemy observers, surveying a distant road crest, would suspect that this apparently innocent private car concealed a hull-down half-track. This SdKfz 250/1, photographed in Italy in 1943, has an overall ochre finish oversprayed with green and brown mottle. (Bundesarchiv)

Army number plate, originally white with a thin black outline, is badly blotched and weathered. The standard red air-recognition flag, containing a black swastika on a white disc, has been secured to the frame aerial.

D: Schwere Panzerspähwagen SdKfz 234/4

This involved mounting the complete 75mm PAK 40 anti-tank gun, less wheels, on a pivot in the centre of the fighting compartment. The effect of this was to turn the vehicle into a wheeled tank destroyer but, once again, full use of the weapon was inhibited by the limited traverse obtainable.

The thickness of hull and turret frontal armour was 30mm; turret side and rear armour was 14.5mm, with 8mm side armour on the hull and 10mm on the rear. The turret was open-topped but was fitted with protective mesh cages similar to those mounted on the 222 light armoured car. Armament consisted of one 20mm cannon mounted co-axially with a 7.92mm machine-gun; radio was now fitted as standard. The vehicle was manned by a crew of four.

E1. SdKfz 250/3 radio halftrack 'Greif' used by Rommel as a command vehicle during his capture of Tobruk, June 1942

In this instance the sand overspray has weathered in vertical streaks which are particularly noticeable on the sides of the vehicle. On the side shown the name 'Greif' (Griffin) is in white outline only, but on the opposite side of the vehicle the white outline is known to have been filled in with red. The Army serial number WH (i.e. Wehrmacht Heer) 937 836 can be seen on the plate at the rear.

E2. SdKfz 261 Kleiner Panzerfunkwagen, unit unknown, Panzerarmee/Afrika; Libya, 1942

The four-man crew of this radio car worked in extremely cramped conditions which left little room for stowage of personal kit, which, in consequence, had to be heaped on the engine deck; a tarpaulin, used to provide shade on protracted outpost duty, is draped across the front of the crew compartment. Fuel jerrycans are carried in a rack on the front of the vehicle, while a further jerrycan, containing either water or lubricating oil, has been lashed to the side armour. A water bottle and several chuggles hang from the side of the crew compartment. The vehicle is finished in plain sand yellow with no trace of erosion, and no markings are visible.

F1. SdKfz 250/10 Self-propelled 37mm Anti-tank Gun, Pz-A-A 'Grossdeutschland', Russia, spring 1943

Very few of these vehicles reached the armoured reconnaissance battalions, but 'Grossdeutschland', being a favoured division, would have received an allocation. The basic colour scheme is Panzer grey with white markings, including the divisional Stalhelm and armoured recon-naissance company symbols on the front of the vehicle.

Halfway down the hull is another marking, which is peculiar to 'GD' vehicles. This may be a diagrammatic representation of the water tower at Storme near Sedan, around which 'Grossdeutschland' fought an epic defensive battle against the French 3eme Division Cuirassée during the breakout from the Meuse bridgeheads.

F2. SdKfz 221 Panzerspähwagen, unit unknown; Russia, winter 1941–1942

During the autumn rains of 1941 and the spring thaw of 1942 movement of any kind for wheeled vehicles on the Eastern Front was extremely difficult if not impossible. In the intervening period hard-frozen ground permitted a degree of movement, and armoured cars were able to perform outpost duties in sometimes Arctic conditions. In addition to the natural snow coverage, the Panzer grey colour scheme of this car has been camouflaged with broad vertical white stripes, roughly applied with brush and whitewash. No markings of any kind are visible.

G1. SdKfz 250/3 radio half-track, unit unknown, Panzergruppe von Kleist; South Russia, late summer 1943

The overall colour scheme of this vehicle is yellow ochre with white markings. These include an outline national cross on the front of the crew compartment, the battle-group's prominent 'K' and, beside the latter, the tactical symbol for the headquarters of the Panzergrenadier regiment to which the vehicle belonged.

G2. SdKfz 232 Schwere Panzerspähwagen (8-rad), Pz-A-A 115; Italy, 1944

The 15.Panzergrenadier-Division was formed in May 1943 from those remnants of 15.Panzer-Division which had managed to avoid the Tunisian débâcle. It served in Italy until September 1944, when it was transferred to the Western Front. Although no markings are visible, this car is known to

A despatch rider catches up with a halted reconnaissance company; his news seems less than popular. In this poor-quality but interesting photo one can see the SdKfz 253 in the foreground – note roof hatch, and rear hull markings including black-white-black non-standard cross. Several figures can he seen to wear the field-grey vehicle uniform with death's-head collar patches. (RAC Tank Museum)

have belonged to the divisional armoured reconnaissance battalion, Pz-A-A 115. In the static warfare conditions prevailing in Italy concealment was all-important and the car's overall yellow ochre finish has been thoroughly blotched in green and dark red-brown to give the dappled effect of sunlight through trees.

INDEX